# Success and Prosperity
## through God's Word

CORNELIUS M. REGAN

WestBow
PRESS
A DIVISION OF THOMAS NELSON

WestBow Press books may be ordered through booksellers or by contacting:

WestBow Press
A Division of Thomas Nelson
1663 Liberty Drive
Bloomington, IN 47403
www.westbowpress.com
1 (866) 928-1240

ISBN: 978-1-4908-1779-8 (sc)
ISBN: 978-1-4908-1778-1 (e)

Library of Congress Control Number: 2013921426

Printed in the United States of America.

WestBow Press rev. date: 11/22/2013

# Acknowledgements

I want to first give honor to God for giving me another chance to do something productive with my life and advance His Kingdom in the process.

To my wife Jeannetta Regan, the woman of my dreams, when God gave me you, He gave me His very best. You are the wind beneath my wings, Jeannetta R. Regan. I thank you for your love that is unconditional and your support of everything I do. I love you, my Dear.

To the Regan and the Massey family, I thank you so much for your love and support. I appreciate everyone who believes in me and I appreciate those who support this ministry and everything we do at CJR Ministries and you know who you are. I thank God for the people that God has placed in my life who allow me to be who I am and to do what God has called me to do.

Thank you, Momma, for your love and support. Proverbs 23:25 says, "Let your father and mother be glad and let her who bore you rejoice." I'm so happy to see you rejoicing—it does me good. I'm so glad I can be a part of the reason for your joy.

# Dedication

This book is dedicated to my Grandma, Mrs. Alene Regan, who made sure the Lord would not forget about me. God kept His promise to you, Grandma. His word won't fail. Your prayers have been answered. Thank you, Grandma, for taking me to church. Hallelujah!

# Contents

# Introduction

I have been walking with the Lord for many years now. I grew up in the church; my Grandmother was faithful in getting us to church on Sunday morning and Wednesday night Bible study. In all of my years of going to the church, I had never read God's word with clarity. I read it before when I was around 17 years old, but they were just words in a book. It wasn't until 1999 that I read it again, but this time I was determined to gain some understanding of what I was reading. Throughout my reading and studying and being around other Christians, I began to see why God's word was so important to a Christian. I began to apply God's word to my life and hide it in my heart that I might not sin against Him. I discovered that God's word could change your life. His word had power—it was infallible, unchanging, and it would stand against anything and anybody. He began to show me that the word had the final authority. It would always have the last say so in any matter. It had the answer to any question I would have in this life. It was the solution to any problem. It could hold our mind together, hold our marriages together and hold our ministries or churches together. God's word could hold our families together. His word could heal a wounded soul or heal a sick diseased body. These are just a few of the many things that the word of God can do if you would turn to it.

Why do I exalt the word so much? Because God said (Psalms 138:2 AMP) that "I will worship toward Your holy temple and praise Your name for Your loving-kindness and for Your truth *and* faithfulness; for You have exalted above all else Your name and Your word *and* You have magnified Your word above all Your name!" We know that there is power in the name of Jesus, so just imagine what God is telling us concerning His holy word. God's word has held my mind together. He has given me peace and joy under circumstances you wouldn't believe. He has held my marriage together in spite of my circumstances. He has blessed us in every area of our lives. He has held my family together. His word has given us the favor of God that He says in His word He would do. He has restored our health and strength, His word has kept us safe from the deceptions of the enemy, from the assaults of the enemy. We have built a ministry through His word. Applying God's word to our lives has opened doors for us that no man can close. I thank God for giving us His word to read and giving us His spirit so that we can understand it and giving us a measure of faith to believe it and the strength and courage to do what it says to do in it. And in following those steps, we will see God's word become a constant reality in our life. His word knows no limitations. The enemy changes, people change, housing markets go down, hard times come to your front door, but through all the vicissitudes of life, you can know God's word will not change. God will do exactly what He says He will do in your life and your circumstances. No matter what the devil or people say, you are who God says you are. So, don't let anyone call you anything when the Bible says He gives you power to become a son of God (John 1:12). (maybe something like "So, don't let anyone make you think you are unworthy when the Bible says He gives you power to become a son of God (John 1:12).

I pray that this book will add to your life and that you will be encouraged to trust in God and lean not unto your own understanding. Acknowledge Him and let Him direct your paths. I can assure that your life will change, your circumstances will get better and your perception will change. If you apply God's word to your life, it will give you a "Complete Makeover."

We at CJR Ministries love you and we care about how your life turns out. Be blessed!

## Success and Prosperity through God's Word

Joshua 1:8 "This book of the law shall not depart out of thy mouth; but thou shalt meditate therein day and night, that thou mayest observe to do according to all that is written therein: for then thou shalt make thy way prosperous, and then thou shalt have good success."

As you begin to read this book, there are a few things that I would like for you to notice. I pray that the Holy Spirit will point out pertinent points- of -view that will be helpful and beneficial to you while on this Christian walk. Let's look at Joshua. He was Moses' predecessor and was appointed by God to usher God's children into the Promised Land. He had many battles ahead of him to fight. He had many obstacles to overcome before he took possession of his inheritance. There is an inheritance laid up for the people of God, but as Joshua, we must take possession of it. Joshua had some assurance that God would be with him as He was with Moses, and that the enemy in front of him would not be able to stand against him. These things are very important when you are going into battle; you have to know God is with you. You have to know that the victory is yours and that your enemy is defeated. But there is one more thing that is a key to guaranteed victory every time, and that is knowing God's word and doing what He says to do.

As we begin to walk with the Lord, it's very important that we know God's word and know what He says in His word concerning us, our family, our finances, our health, destiny, purpose, mind, our past, and our total being. As we look back in the first nine verses of Joshua, chapter one, we see that God tells Joshua to be strong three times. The number nine means "wholeness." Jesus died on the ninth hour which tells me He made man whole and restored man to completeness in the spiritual realm. However, man also had to go through a process in the natural to be able to walk in what God had already done for him at Calvary. Just as told to Joshua in Deut. 9:1-3, God tells Israel:

> "Thou art to pass over Jordan this day, to go in to possess nations greater and mightier than thyself, cities great and fenced up to heaven, ²A people great and tall, the children of the Anakims, whom thou knowest, and of whom thou hast heard say, Who can stand before the children of Anak! ³Understand therefore this day, that the LORD thy God is he which goeth over before thee; as a consuming fire he shall destroy them, and he shall bring them down before thy face: so shalt thou drive them out, and destroy them quickly, as the LORD hath said unto thee."

God tells them that I have gone before you as your forerunner (Hebrews 6:20). He has taken away the enemies power, not to say that the enemy doesn't have power, but he is powerless against the believer. Praise God!

If God is for us, who can be against us? No one can stand against the man with whom God is standing. Three times God tells Joshua to "be strong," so let us look at the number three which represents the resurrection which also means victory over sin, death, oppression, depression, sickness, and poverty. He says to Joshua in verses 6, 7 and 9 to "be strong." That tells me that God wants the believer strong in every area of his life, which includes 1. Physical strength, 2. Spiritual strength and 3. Emotional strength, which includes the mind, human will, and feelings. Hear me child of God! You must be strong in these areas so that you can fulfill your purpose in this life. Your gift is not enough by itself. For example, high blood pressure will slow you down. It has the potential to stop you completely. Exercise and right eating is important. I know you are probably wondering what this has to do with my purpose? Child of God, it has everything to do with it because an unhealthy person is not functioning in the capacity in which God has intended him to function because the body is weak. A lot of us take the scripture in I Timothy 4:8 out of context that says "bodily exercise profits little" but nonetheless there is a profit in it. So let's get all the benefits of being a child of the King.

God showed Joshua in verse 8 that his faith and trust must be in His word. The Book of Law—it is the way to success and prosperity. He tells Joshua that the Law shall not depart out of his mouth. God is saying to Joshua to always say what the Law (the word) says and keep the word on your tongue. In this battle against the forces of darkness, the word of God coming out of your mouth will be your greatest weapon. The word is called a two-edged sword for a good reason. God is saying to His children to never agree with the enemy concerning your health, finances, your future, nor your family. The enemy will tell you that your health will fail you because everyone in the family has cancer, but you must tell him that Christ has redeemed you from the curse of the law and that by His stripes you were healed. The devil will tell you that your family members will never get saved, but you must tell him that God is not willing that any should perish but that all would come to repentance and that God is touching them by His power right now in Jesus name! The enemy will tell you that the economy is bad and you will always struggle financially, but God says He will supply all your needs and that He is your shepherd and you shall not want. Satan will tell the inmate that he is never getting out of prison, but God says He came to set the captives free and loose those that are bound in the prison. I am sure you get my point by now child of God. Never look back at neither the circumstances nor the situation and agree with it. Keep on saying what God says because His word is what is going to stand forever. His word will not return unto Him void. Job 22:21 says, "Agree with God and be at peace; thereby good may come unto you."

God goes on to say to meditate on the Word day and night. The word "meditate" means in Hebrew to ponder, imagine, and mutter the word of God. You must imagine yourself in good health; draw an image of yourself getting the victory over the situation at hand. This must be who you are. His word must become a part of you. There has to be some intimacy with Christ in order to bear fruit, this is why God says day and night your consecration should never be broken! He also tells us to do what He says to do. This is imperative for victory—your total obedience to the word of God. As you understand God's word through studying, you will notice that God stands behind His word no matter what! That is why we must obey it, no matter what! And then He shall make your way prosperous and you will have good success.

Let's look at these two words that we all love: Prosperous and Success. Everyone desires to be prosperous and successful. I haven't met many men or women who didn't desire to be successful and prosperous in this life. Prosperous—to be prosperous in Hebrew means "tsalach" which means prosperity, to push forward in various senses, to be profitable. I love these meanings because they coincide with what every believer desires in his heart. He desires to push forward in every area of his life and in his career. I know because nobody wants to stay a janitor, he wants one day to at least own a cleaning company. In law enforcement, we want to advance to higher levels and that is what God wants for us. It's God's will that we advance in our health, our marriage, our education, and you fill in the blanks. It's not always the bigger paycheck, because the bigger bank account doesn't make me successful—it's the achievement of one's goals and dreams. It's doing the things that live up with what our gifts and talents are; our doing what we enjoy and for what we have a passion. Doing this is true prosperity for the child of God. In Hebrew, the word Success is "sakal" which means to be an expert, to prosper, to be wise, to have wisdom, to have understanding. To be an expert means to be a master at your craft. To be wise and to have wisdom is powerful and we will never be successful if we continue to make foolish decisions. Why? Because foolish choices set us back in life and bad choices cause us to go backwards instead of forward. This is why Psalms 90:12 says "teach us to number our days so that we may apply our hearts onto wisdom." The scripture is saying that we only have a limited time on this earth and we must use the wisdom of God so that we can make every day count. God desires for us to be blessed in all areas of life. Now we see the importance of the word and obeying it. His word is His wisdom that will set you on a very prosperous journey if you obey it. Your prosperity and success comes through your obedience to God's Holy Word.

*Hebrews 4:12*
*Gal 3:13*
*Isaiah 53:5*
*Philippians 4:16*
*Psalms 23:1*
*Isaiah 61*
*II Peter 3:9*
*Isaiah 55:11*

# Chapter 2
# The Crucifixion

Joshua 5:2-3 "At that time the LORD said unto Joshua, Make thee sharp knives, and circumcise again the children of Israel the second time. ³And Joshua made him sharp knives, and circumcised the children of Israel at the hill of the foreskins." God is saying to Joshua that there must be an operation; a circumcision has to be performed on the eight day after the child was born, and my covenant shall be in your flesh for an everlasting covenant (Genesis 17:12-13). Circumcision signified that the infant was being taken into the covenant community. Therefore, this practice was carefully observed. An uncircumcised person was considered to be a heathen. To be uncircumcised would mean you are not under the covenant which means you are separated from God. So circumcision is an extremely delicate operation. How does this relate to you now that you are an adult and/or woman? As you are walking with the Lord and you are talking about Purpose and Destiny, there will have to be a cutting of the

flesh before you enter the promise land; there has to be an operation of the heart and doing away with our old nature. This is important because the flesh and the spirit are at war with one another, and if you don't crucify your flesh, it will hinder you from progressing into the things that God has for you. This is serious! People will tell you that your obedience to God and saying "no" to the flesh is overrated, but the devil is a lie! God says in Malachi 3:6, "I am the Lord, I change not." God's word is consistent with His nature and His nature is holiness and righteousness. Your flesh has the potential to destroy you and cancel your appointment with destiny. Cutting of the flesh is not an easy process, but it is necessary! You can never be all God called you to be if your flesh is still dominating you. Paul says in I Corinthians 9:27 about keeping His body "under subjection, lest that by any means, when I have preached to others," he would not be disqualified. Yes, your flesh will disqualify you from the Promised Land. God makes no mistakes. His process is a must if you are talking about getting the one hundred fold lifestyle that God has promised us. There are no shortcuts to the Promised Land, so stop looking! Ask Moses. He couldn't enter the land because of his anger in which the flesh took control of him and caused him to disobey God by hitting the rock instead of speaking to it as God had instructed him.

Internal anger issues are works of the flesh. Now how do I crucify my flesh? Now that I understand, I must get on the operating table. First, I must understand that the One who is doing the cutting is a master physician. God Himself is going to perform the surgery. Only until I agree that this surgery is mandatory to making me the man or woman that God has called me to be, will I not be set back or hindered anymore. For the Word of God is quick and powerful and sharper than any two-edged sword, piercing even to the dividing asunder of soul and spirit, and of the joints and marrows, and is a discerner of thoughts and intents of the heart. Let's clarify something that I deem to be important because I know some of you are wondering how can God be the physician and how the Bible says the word of God is going to do the cutting? Let's look at St. John 1:1: "In the beginning was the Word, and the Word was with God, and the Word was God." We see here that the Word and God are the same. Now that we have that clear, let's proceed with the operation. God is going into the soul which is your mind, your will, and your emotions—right? He is getting your spirit right because this is how we relate to God—spirit to spirit.

God is going into the joints and marrow, into the bone structure of a man as He did with Jacob in Genesis 32:25. Jacob had to go through the surgery in order to go further into God. After his surgery, his walk changed, his name changed and his fate changed. Had he not had surgery before he met Esau, he would have been doomed, but when a man's ways pleases the Lord, he makes his enemies to be at peace with him. God changed Jacob and instead of Esau seeing Jacob, the con man, Esau saw Israel, a man who had power with God. And man has prevailed. Praise God! Once God deals with a man, he deals with every issue. He is the great physician. He leaves no stones unturned. He makes a man whole so we as His children and won't lack anything.

*Galatians 5:17*
*Hebrews 4:12*
*Proverbs 16:7*

# Chapter 3
# Seven Times, Lord

Joshua 6:1-2 "Now Jericho was straitly shut up because of the children of Israel: none went out, and none came in. And the LORD said unto Joshua, See, I have given into thine hand Jericho, and the king thereof, and the mighty men of valour." Jericho was a high walled city and to look at it, it would actually frighten a man who is not sure of himself and sure of his God's power to penetrate any situation or circumstance that stands between him and his destiny. Remember God and His word are the same and the word is impregnable which means it cannot be penetrated, therefore, it is God that does the penetrating. That's why David says through Him, "I could run through a troop and leap over a wall." Jeremiah says in the 23$^{rd}$ chapter v. 29 that the "word is like a fire, saith the Lord, and like a hammer that breaks in pieces the rock" (of most stubborn resistance), nothing and no one can stand against God and His anointed. And God goes on to tell Joshua to perceive because He has given

Jericho into his hand. What God is saying to us is that He has given us the victory but we must see it with eyes of faith. We must be able to see into the spiritual realm. God tells us to see into the spiritual because when you are facing giants, walls and difficult circumstances, you have to be able to see God in it in order to conquer it. It is impossible to conquer your enemies with your eyes focused on the problem instead of the answer.

The Lord then tells Joshua to go around the city once for six days and on the seventh day, go around seven times and blow the trumpets. The number seven means complete. God is saying, "I'm going to give you complete victory." But Joshua has a role to play in order to get the victory over Jericho. Yes, we have to do something; victory doesn't just come because God hasn't designed it that way. Even God worked. He was speaking the world into existence and that is what we are required to do in certain situations. As is this situation, we are required to obey God and have faith in His word by doing exactly what He says. Doing exactly what God says is what secures our victory, but we must believe God even when His ways and methods seem strange. God's ways are not like our ways, child of God. So, it is best to obey Him and trust Him with the outcome. Don't question it or second guess it, just do it! God says when you go around the walls the seventh time and shout, the wall is going to fall flat! Here is another key factor in this passage. We shall not shout or make any noise until He says so. God knows how we are and if He doesn't give us specific instructions not to say anything, we will be murmuring and complaining and speaking doubt, and boy, we specialize in talking ourselves out of the victory that has been given to us. So, take this as a warning to you if you are not saying what the word says. Don't say anything. God is instructing us to keep walking no matter what. Could He have brought victory in the second trip around the wall? Of course, but He has a plan and the number seven is His number for completing the job. Now we must shout! I'd like to think that shouting is a form of praise and we know the power that praise has. Praise and shouting moves God into action on our behalf. God loves a person that will praise Him in any situation.

Your praise moves our Father into action. Ask Paul and Silas. Their praise caused the foundation of a prison to shake and break the chains off of all the inmates. Our brother, King Jehoshaphat, went into singing as he was instructed by God to do and God caused the enemies of Jehoshaphat to kill themselves. Their singing, shouting and praising confused the enemies. Why is God so excited about your praise? One reason is because it shows complete trust in His ability to bring you into victory from defeat: from prison to freedom, from sickness to health and from poverty to wealth. A man's victory is often times not found—not in his wallet, not in his bank account, not in his associates, but in his praise to the God of Heaven and Earth. When you can praise Him before the victory, you can be assured victory is not far behind the praise. We are showing God that even though I'm in a mess, I believe You are going to turn it around for me, as with Joshua. You may not do it the first or second time, but if I keep on going, You will turn it around for me. Praise God! And the wall fell flat as God said they would. His power was displayed. This is what every child of God desires and that is to see His power manifested. And if you obey, trust, have faith, and praise, your manifestation is sure!

## First Fruit

Jericho falls. Joshua 6:18 "And ye, in any wise keep yourselves from the accursed thing, lest ye make yourselves accursed, when ye take of the accursed thing, and make the camp of Israel a curse, and trouble it." In this text, we see God speaking through Joshua about taking the accursed thing. The accursed thing is something that should have been destroyed. It is a doomed object, it was appointed to utter destruction. Now God says in v.19 "all the silver, and gold, and vessels of brass and iron, are consecrated unto the LORD: they shall come into the treasury of the LORD." These vessels of iron and gold are the First Fruits. Thus the first battles and first fruits belong to the Lord. It should be our pleasure to give God His due, all the time. He should always get His tenth of our income first. These are good principles that keep us in the flow of God's blessings.

*Psalms 18:29*

# Chapter 4
# Accursed Thing

Joshua 7:1 "But the children of Israel committed a trespass in the accursed thing: for Achan, the son of Carmi, the son of Zabdi, the son of Zerah, of the tribe of Judah, took of the accursed thing: and the anger of the LORD was kindled against the children of Israel." Achan had taken the accursed thing and then he had troubled the camp. The children of Israel had brought judgment on themselves by their disobedience to what God had said. They were on their way to fight Ai. Ai meant "little one" and because of their size, Joshua only sent two or three thousand men to fight in this battle. But to their surprise, they began to be overthrown by the enemy and began being chased. Never underestimate the enemy because when he comes at you, he is coming with everything he has in his arsenal. Israel was being chased and Ai chased Israel all the way to Shebarim and smote them there. Let's look at the word Shebarim, it has a very significant meaning. Shebarim means "breaches."

God was about to show Israel the reason for their defeat. There was a breach in their relationship to God. There was a gap, a violation in the contract between Israel and God. Gap and violation are the words Webster uses for the definition of breach. Israel had violated the commandments of God and it caused a gap between them. (Isaiah 59:2) "But your iniquities have separated between you and your God, and your sins have hid His face from you, that He will not hear." Sin separates a man from God. God had told Joshua that no man should stand before Him, but the prerequisite was that they would do as God told them. If they obeyed God, He said He would go with them wherever they went and especially in battle. That's a promise from God that I've learned to appreciate because we need God to be in every area of our life. We need Him in our marriage, personal life, on the job, in the market, at the park, the cookout, in this prison, and in the court case. Wherever we go, we need the Lord!

# Chapter 5
# Sin in the House

Joshua 7:6 "And Joshua rent his clothes, and fell to the earth upon his face before the ark of the LORD until the eventide, he and the elders of Israel, and put dust upon their heads." Joshua did what all God's people should do when we experience something on our journey that is inconsistent with the nature of our God. He and the Elders humbled themselves before the God. The Bible says they fell to the earth. Sometimes you have to fall on your face before the Lord until you get an answer or some peace about your situation. That's what the Bible means when it says He stayed before the Ark until eventide. He stayed in the face of God until God told him to get up because Israel had sinned and had transgressed the covenant which God had commanded them. They broke the contract, the agreement, because of their sin. They had taken the accursed thing and tried to cover it up with their stuff. Joshua had gone before the Lord and then he went before the people and started

asking questions and with the guidance of the Lord, he knew which way to look because God had shown him that Israel had sinned. It's the same with us in the spirit. When God makes us promises and we begin to experience defeat of some kind, we know that somebody has gotten out of order, someone has violated God's covenant. It was an act of deception with Achan. Take heed! God is serious about His covenant. When we enter into covenant with God, his strength, protection, wisdom and knowledge is ours. And because they had broken the covenant they could not stand before their enemies. The Bible says in Deut. 28:25, "If we disobey Him, we shall be smitten before our enemies. We shall come one way and flee seven ways." And this is exactly what happened to Israel. Ai chased and smote them.

What is God saying to His children? Your power is in your obedience. Let's go back to the beginning with Adam. He had everything. He was perfect; he had dominion, authority, and increase. Adam had it all until he disobeyed God's word. In one act of disobedience, his authority had been transferred from his hands to Satan's. That goes for any and all of us who disobey God. We lose our power. Achan represents sin inside of the body. So what is God saying to us? He is saying you got the big sins out of the way, but what about the craftiness, hidden dishonesty, lust in your heart, wickedness inside that no one can see and pride (that silent murderer). Yes, these are the things that are holding you back. They are hindering you from going into your destiny. These are the things that are causing you to be late for your appointment with destiny. You may be able to hide them from man, but your secret sins are open before God and as we can see, they will hinder your advancement. As God told Joshua, remove the accursed thing. You should disassociate yourselves with those sins and get back on track. Repent and rid yourselves of the things and then proceed with your journey towards your goals, dreams and the vision that God has given you for your life.

## The Consequences of Sin

Achan's sin was exposed because of the defeat of the Israelites in battle against Ai. God had promised them victory everywhere they went, but they had experienced defeat, so Joshua inquired about it to God and God exposed the sin of deception. Now when we choose to disobey God in any manner, there is a penalty that has to be paid. God doesn't overlook sin. He wouldn't be a just God if He did. Some of our sins would bring greater penalties than others, but nonetheless, judgment is coming. Achan was a part of Israel and Israel was a peculiar people destined for the promises of God. Jesus died for us all that we may experience God's very best for our lives, but Achan chose to disobey God and it cost him his life and the lives of others connected to him. The Bible says that "the wages of sin is death!" Because of Achan's sin, all of his cattle, his wife, his sons, his daughters, all whom were innocent, were sentenced to death. Achan's entire family was punished because of the acts of the father. Listen people of God, you will affect everyone you love in a very negative way when you choose to rebel against the commandments of our God. Your sins will bring misery, pain, and sometimes death to your families. Our sins have killed our marriages, our relationships with our children;

some have even killed our children's opportunities of getting degrees or attending college. Sin has a way of killing our dreams. Many men are serving long prison sentences and have lost the chance of ever being a great father to their children or being a wonderful husband to their wives. Some may never be the man or woman that God has chosen them to be as well.

Making a righteous decision not only applies to married people with families, but it also pertains to you single men and women who are raising children on their own. Be wise in your dealings! Don't live a compromising lifestyle! Know that whatever man or women you choose to marry, this marriage will affect your children's lives as well. So don't be so selfish in your dealings by making decisions and not considering the ones that it will affect. Don't get so caught up in what you want so bad that you forget that every decision you make will affect those closest to you. Before you make your next major decision, please take the time out to look into the eyes of your husband's, wife's or children's eyes and know that this choice will affect them one way or the other.

*Isaiah 54:17*

# Chapter 6
# He is Our Battle Fighter

Joshua 9:1-2 "And it came to pass, when all the kings which were on this side Jordan, in the hills, and in the valleys, and in all the coasts of the great sea over against Lebanon, the Hittite, and the Amorite, the Canaanite, the Perizzite, the Hivite, and the Jebusite, heard thereof; ²That they gathered themselves together, to fight with Joshua and with Israel, with one accord." In my research, I came across some very significant information about our enemies so that you will be able to identify the enemy in this day and time. It is important to know your enemy by its name so you can call that demon out. Further in the passage, I identify the devils Joshua and Israel were up against. As you can see from these passages, it is clear that our battle will get more intense at times, the closer we get to our destiny. People that don't even care for each other will become comrades just to stop you. Look at the Pharisees and Suducees. They joined forces and tried to hinder Jesus from doing the will of the

Father. What the enemy doesn't know is that every time he tries to hinder us, he's only pushing us into prayer, praise, fasting, and seeking God as never before. All we have to do is remain obedient to God and no weapon formed against us shall prosper. Just check God's track record! It is an awesome record as proven in the story of Joseph.

In the story of Joseph, God had shown Joseph his destiny in a dream, and the Bible says that his brothers envied him. The enemy attempted to stop God's plan for Joseph by using his brothers to sell him in to slavery. They began to plot in ways to kill Joseph (Genesis 37:18), but God was with Joseph. This should alert you that the enemy is trying to kill you. He not only wants to paralyze your progress, but he wants to annihilate you from the face of the earth. Thank God that Judah stepped in! We know that Judah means praise and God is trying to tell us that the only thing that can save you from the hands of your enemies is praise and that's why we have to praise God. Your praise frustrates the plans of the enemy. If I were you, I would praise Him right now for the next five minutes! After that, Joseph was sold into slavery and delivered into a foreign land, but God was the Rock in the weary land. Praise God for being my Rock. Joseph was in this land as a slave working for Potiphar, the captain of the guard, an officer of Pharoah. God never left Joseph's side and he had favor in this land and the land prospered because Joseph was in the land. Everything he touched succeeded and flourished in his hands. We must keep in mind that the enemy was persistent in his plan to destroy this young man before he walked into the promises of God for his life. Joseph began to shine in this place and everyone took notice. God said we are the light of the world, a city set on a hill that cannot be hidden; and when God's glory is on your life, you become very attractive because the glory of God is beautiful. The anointing is very attractive. And here comes Potiphar's wife. We know that she was a beautiful woman who could bring Joseph to a place of honor because of whom she was and her connections. Her husband was the captain directly King Pharaoh; therefore, she had money and political ties. She had everything a man needed, especially under Joseph's circumstances. He was young and needed a friend like her. Watch out for the enemy because he plots on the vulnerable and that was our young brother, Joseph. He was in a vulnerable situation. When the money is funny, don't compromise; when the spouse is acting up, don't compromise; when life seems like it's not going to get any better, hold on to the dream or the vision that God has placed in your heart because He is faithful and He can't lie. I know it hurts and I know it's rough, and I've been there, but trust me, it gets better. God's plan for your life will come to pass. I want to share this secret with you; every promise of God has a plan attached to it! And when the plan and process is fulfilled, the promise will be fulfilled as well. Before the fulfillment of God's promise over Joseph's life, there was a process that he had to go through. Nevertheless, Joseph didn't allow the enemy to distract him from doing the right thing in remaining faithful to God. Joseph was a man of integrity and he didn't compromise in the middle of the test. He wore his armor, and the two shields operating at that time were the breastplate of righteousness and the belt of truth. He did the right thing by refusing to lay with his master's wife and to sin against God. Joseph showed that he had integrity and could be trusted at the same time. Now why do I say to you that these are important? You must have your armor on because the enemy is trying to sabotage your life by getting you to sell out to him and sin against God. When we sin, the weapon that was set out to destroy has room to do what it was set out to do in our lives, so you must put on righteousness and the belt of truth as Joseph did because these are the protectors against the enemy's attacks. Joseph didn't sell out and he was punished for it and was sentenced to life in prison. Let's look a little further, Joseph was a Hebrew slave and by law he was supposed to get the death penalty BUT GOD HAS A PLAN and he cannot die! He has to walk into his destiny, so he goes to prison and God is with him in the prison and he becomes overseer in the prison over all the inmates. Look at God's favor on his life. It doesn't matter what you do—if God is for us, He will favor you anywhere you may find yourself. After Joseph had spent enough time in prison, God was about to bring the dream to pass in his life. God caused two men that were in prison with Joseph to have a dream. I can't help but to tell you that Joseph was on a divine timetable. God's vision for your life is at an appointed time. Ecclesiastes 3:1 says, "To everything there is a season, and a time for every purpose under the heaven." So, that thing that God has promised to do in your life will manifest at the right time, which is God's time, so just hold on! And "though it tarry it will surely come to pass, wait for it" (Habakkuk 2:3). Joseph was able to interpret the dreams and it wasn't long after he revealed the dream that one of the prisoners, the cupbearer, was restored back to his position. While in position, Pharoah had a dream that he couldn't interpret. So you can guess who the cupbearer summoned for the interpretation. You are right—Joseph. NOW it was time for Joseph to take his position just as God had revealed to him in a dream many years ago. Joseph became the prime minister of Egypt, second in command over the whole country. He went straight out of prison as the scripture says "he cometh out prison to reign" (Ecclesiastes 4:14). I didn't mean to go through the whole story of Joseph's life, but I was compelled to do so because his story is so amazing and it shows it doesn't matter how low you go in this world. If God has spoken something into your spirit or if He has showed you anything, God will show up to bring it to pass just as He promised He would.

Look at Jesus and His location and look at Joshua. As long as they stayed obedient, they couldn't be stopped. God will fight your battles. Jesus is seated in Glory and Joshua into the Promised Land. So, don't be afraid of the size of the army. God and you are always the majority! See II Kings 6:16 when Elisha and his servant were surrounded by a great army and the servant was afraid. The man of God, Elisha said, "Fear not, for they that be with us are more than they that be with them." Elisha understood who God was, and he knew that as long as God was with him, no one could stand against him. For all my brothers and sisters—never engage in anything without the Lord.

St. John 15:5 "I am the vine, ye are the branches: He that abideth in me, and I in him, the same bringeth forth much fruit: for without me ye can do nothing." You may be saying to yourself that you can do some things without God, but as you walk with the Lord, you will learn that your success in life depends on your connection to God. This is why the significance in the names of your enemies is so important. Hitite means to break down by violence; confusion or fear. Your enemy seeks to break the believers down by confusion, violence, and fear. So when there is confusion in your life, it is the enemy. When there is confusion in your marriage or on your job, or confusion in making a decision, go to God because the enemy is the author of confusion. But the way of the righteous is made plain. God will bring you clarity on your journey as you seek Him. Then there is fear—we know fear is not from God because God doesn't give us the spirit of fear, but of power, love and a sound mind. You must overcome fear in this journey because fear will paralyze you. God often times leads us into new territory and if we are afraid, we will not move when God says move. Our fear must be conquered.

Amorite means pride, prominence. We know how God feels about pride—he hates it. The reason why pride must be conquered is because it comes before a fall. Your pride will bring you low. It has the potential to destroy you. A proud man will not listen to God or anyone else. He exalts himself above others and because of his arrogance; he sets himself up for all types of disasters and pitfalls. God cannot use a man that is prideful and neither can He exalt him because God exalts those who humble themselves under His mighty hand and He will exalt them in due time which is His divine time and that's God's order and it doesn't change.

The word prominence is given in Webster as eminent; a position of superiority or distinction. We cannot be seeking glory for ourselves. Remember Jesus emptied Himself and became of no reputation. He didn't seek position or to be put on a pedestal and neither should we. Canaanite means peddler, merchant or to humiliate. The enemy will try to sell you his lies. And if we buy into his conniving ways, we will be humiliated; shame will be your promotion. Perizzites means to be rustic or squatter; rustic means to be simple and if you are simple-minded you will go for anything. Romans 16:18 talks about how good words and sound speech deceive the hearts of the simple. So prove all things, hold fast to that which is good. Squatter is an example of the enemy squatting on territory that doesn't belong to him. The Perrizites were resting and squatting in a land that God had promised to His own people, and they had to go in and possess it. It's also like a person going inside of a vacant house or while someone is away and staying in it like it is their house. It doesn't belong to them. That is what society calls a squatter and that is what the Perrizites were in the Promised Land.

Hivites means showers of life, rivers or serpents. The enemy can give the appearance of life. He comes as an angel of light so you must have the spirit of discernment so he doesn't get the advantage over you. Jebusites means those who will be trodden down which says to us no matter what the enemy's tactics, the end for him is defeat! Praise God! These are some of the enemies you will face on the way to your destiny. They will submit to the believer who fights the good fight of faith in the name of Jesus. Now, when you see these things in you or around you, you'll have a point of reference. And now you know how to move past them and overcome them.

# Chapter 7
# Great Faith

Joshua 10:11 "And it came to pass, as they fled from before Israel, and were in the going down to Beth-horon, that the LORD cast down great stones from heaven upon them unto Azekah, and they died: they were more which died with hailstones than they whom the children of Israel slew with the sword." The Lord intervened and destroyed the enemy with hailstones. Your faith in God will activate His power on your behalf. As we see in this scripture, it isn't the might of Joshua that slew the enemy because it is not by might, nor by power. "It is by My spirit," says the Lord, that your enemy will be defeated so that you cannot say that you have done something with your own strength and try to take God's glory.

Joshua 10:12-13 "Then spake Joshua to the LORD in the day when the LORD delivered up the Amorites before the children of Israel, and he said in the sight of Israel,

Sun, stand thou still upon Gibeon; and thou, Moon, in the valley of Ajalon. [13]And the sun stood still, and the moon stayed, until the people had avenged themselves upon their enemies. Is not this written in the book of Jasher? So the sun stood still in the midst of heaven, and hasted not to go down about a whole day." Joshua proceeded into battle, but I want to point something out that he did that many of us do not do. And the Bible says Joshua spoke to the Lord. He had learned through experience that doing things without consulting the Lord is not wisdom. When the Bible says "trust in the LORD with all thine heart; and lean not unto thine own understanding. In all thy ways acknowledge Him, and He shall direct thy paths." It is important to understand this because it will very well determine the outcome of your situation. Sometimes we are too confident in ourselves, our gifts, and our talents alone. There is power in agreement. Let's look at how God and man worked in harmony with each other and a great victory was won. The miracles occurred. Let's look at King David, Moses, Elijah and many more of God's people that cooperated with God. When they did, the blessing came. So when Joshua finished his conversation with God, he spoke to the elements of nature in the sight of Israel and the sun obeyed him. Notice it obeyed the man who spoke with the authority that he had been given from God. You see, Joshua was in battle and he needed more light in order to come out victorious. We have authority as believers in God, and many believers don't understand the authority that they have in Christ. Jesus said in St. John 14:12, "Verily, verily, I say unto you, He that believeth on me, the works that I do shall he do also; and greater works than these shall he do; because I go

31

unto my Father." What works did He do? He spoke to dead bodies and they came back to life. He spoke to the wind storms and they obeyed Him. He defied the laws of nature by walking on water. He walked in His authority and so can we as we stay in communion with the Father. As you can see here, the key to your success is your relationship with God. Joshua spoke to the sun in the sight of Israel which is significant because God wants us to see that as long as we have faith and we are in His will, we can have what we say. Many times we are ashamed to declare and decree things in the sight of people because we feel we will be embarrassed or shamed. But God will not shame those who trust and obey Him. When Jesus spoke to Lazarus, He spoke in front of everyone and the dead body had to submit to the Word that came out of His mouth. The Bible says that life and death are in the power of your tongue and those who love it will eat the fruit thereof. We have absolute authority to say what God's Word says concerning any situation. When the enemy attacks your money, you can go to God and find out what he has to say about your finances and start decreeing God's Word. And God will supply all of your needs according to His riches in glory by Christ Jesus.

Faith was another key that Joshua used, and his faith in God released the power of God because the sun did what the man of God commanded it to do. The Bible says according to your faith be it done unto you. He had to believe that the thought of speaking to the sun and expecting it to stand in its place was from the Lord. Often times God places things in our spirits and they seem far-fetched, and when we tune in and do what we sense the spirit is telling us to do, we will experience the miraculous. Many times we as believers don't experience God in greater dimensions because we only can move God's hand by our faith. It takes faith to decree to the elements of the world and stand in that faith until they do what you have commanded them to do. You, child of God, as Joshua did, need a miracle from the Lord in your circumstances, whatever they may be, and I say "they" because nothing is impossible with God. He can do anything and He will do it for you, but it's your faith, child of God, that will cause Him to move on your behalf. And as Joshua did to get his miracle, you must also speak to the Lord. Once you have heard from Him concerning the situation at hand, you must speak to the mountain (whatever that mountain may be) and continue to speak to it until it is removed and your promise comes to pass in your life.

The Bible says the sun stood still a whole day so that Joshua and Israel could go into the Promised Land. He depended on a word from the Lord as we must when we are talking about purpose, destiny, success, and prosperity because it comes to you through your meditation on God's word; listening for His voice, and doing what He says to do. God is not slack concerning His promises. He is never late. The vision is for an appointed time. I know you are wondering why God answered Joshua so quickly and sometimes we wait months and years to see miracles from God. Joshua needed God right then and if God didn't come to his side, they would have lost the battle, and what God told Joshua in the beginning would have been a lie! There have been times in your life where God answered as soon as you prayed. Oh, you remember that time you needed the money for that bill; the time you were feeling bad and the pain went away immediately; a time when that situation had you so stretched out and was turned around with one phone call or text; or that one whisper from the Lord and all of your fears were suddenly gone. Yes, my sisters and brothers, we have been there. Now there are also the situations that took longer and there are ones that haven't been answered yet. But listen to me! The flower fades and the grass withers, but the Word of the Lord shall stand forever. Everything and everybody else may fall through, but God's Word shall stand. His Word will not return unto Him void and when it comes out of your mouth it will accomplish what He said it would do.

*Proverbs 3:5-6*
*Zachariah 4:6*
*Isaiah 40:8*
*Isaiah 55:11*

# Chapter 8
# Destiny

Joshua 11:19 "There was not a city that made peace with the children of Israel, save the Hivites, the inhabitants of Gibeon: all other they took in battle." More often than ever, the enemy is occupying territory that belongs to us believers, just as all the tribes were squatting on the children of Israel's land that God had promised them. And as you can see in the story, Joshua had to take in battle the majority of the land. So please understand Paul when he says in I Timothy 6:12, "Fight the good fight of faith, lay hold on eternal life, whereunto thou art also called, and hast professed a good profession before many witnesses." Yes, the enemy is sitting on some things that God says are yours, but you must be prepared to go into the enemy's camp and take your freedom and take back your child, your mind, your life, your career, your family, your peace, your joy or your house. The devil is a thief and robber and he has stolen from the believer, but he can only keep what you allow him to keep. And that is the

good news. David's men and their families were kidnapped and taken captive, and he was drowning in sorrow as we all do when we mess up bad or we lose BIG!

The Bible says David was greatly distressed, but he encouraged himself in the Lord his God. And that is what we must do. We must get up from the pity party, stop crying and get back in battle mode. Before David went to God, he went to the priest for the Ephod. The Ephod was a religious garment worn by priests that covered their back and their breast. David knew that he had to go before God correctly, and he did. He got the word from the Lord and he recovered ALL that the enemy had stolen from him. You see what David and Joshua did; they laid hold of what was theirs. They pursued until they possessed what was their God-given inheritance. Many of us want everything easy, but it's not like that always. The Kingdom of Heaven suffereth violence and the violent take it by force. Sometimes you have to pray all night in the spirit. You have to decree things over and over again when nothing is happening and you are looking and sounding crazy, but you are taking it by force. Get your word from the Lord concerning your situation and go get your inheritance—go and get you stuff. This is not a time to be timid—you have entered a battle since the day of your conversion from sin to Christ. What some of you need to do is roll up your sleeves and fight this fight of faith as God gives the orders because your success depends on your obedience to God.

Your success in every area of your life depends on your faith in God's Word. And your faith has the ability to lay ahold of God's promises until they come to pass. I've learned through personal experience that I don't have to live a defeated life, not in order to stay in victory. I must stay close to my God and be obedient to His Word. The times that I have ever experienced defeat, I was in control and leaving God out. I was making decisions and hoping He would get involved with my stuff and give me the outcome I wanted. Does that sound familiar? I've learned to pray according to His will and when I do that, I have an assurance that I cannot be denied.

## Learning God's Will

What is God's will? God's will is His Word. As you go into His Word and pray over a situation, He will reveal the answer to you. You must have faith in what He has promised will come to pass in your life. All the promises of God are Yea and Amen. The enemy will fight you all the way in your mind, body, and soul but you must be equipped in those areas as well. Satan will tell you that you won't get well; you will always be broke; you are always going to have a bad attitude; that disease runs in the family. The enemy is lying to you. He lied to Eve and she believed him, then look at what happened. They got kicked out of the Garden of Eden. Don't believe the lie. Your life depends on it. Your children's welfare depends on it; your marriage depends on it; your destiny depends on it. Everything that is contrary to God's Word is from the devil and you don't have to agree with him. You have the authority to cast down thoughts that he brings in your mind, imaginations, and any images that he places in your mind and any reasoning that exalts itself against the knowledge of God and bring them into captivity. Satan is always trying to exalt his teachings above God's Word but you can cast them down as soon as he shows you or tells you something that doesn't line up with the Word. Now you know that life of mediocrity, living from check to check all your life, alone for the rest of your life, taking medication for the rest of your life, in captivity for life, all these things are not from God. They are the devil's lies. It's time to get a new image, some new thoughts, and some new ideas about your life. And you must go to the Word of God because the world doesn't offer hope anymore. It offers stress, mess, and confusion. Therefore, if you're going to be successful, you must go to God and trust him with every fiber of your being. Your prosperity lies in the hands of a loving Father who has created you for success. He created you to be the best in your arena; to worship and honor Him all the way to the top.

*II Corinthians 10:34*

# Chapter 9
# More of God

II Chronicles 26:1-5 "Then all the people of Judah took Uzziah, who was sixteen years old, and made him king in the room of his father Amaziah. ²He built Eloth, and restored it to Judah, after that the king slept with his fathers. ³Sixteen years old was Uzziah when he began to reign, and he reigned fifty and two years in Jerusalem. His mother's name also was Jecoliah of Jerusalem. ⁴And he did that which was right in the sight of the LORD, according to all that his father Amaziah did. ⁵And he sought God in the days of Zechariah, who had understanding in the visions of God: and as long as he sought the LORD, God made him to prosper." Here we have our word again prosper. It is the same exact word in the Hebrew language as prosperous in Joshua 1:8 which means to advance. Now let's look at the advancement of this young king who shows his immaturity in the things of God. It would be fair to say that he didn't know a lot, but yet he did what was right in the sight of the Lord. He knew little and he was obedient to the things that he knew. This is very important in your walk with the Lord, especially to those who may have known God in only a short time. I charge you in the name of Jesus to be faithful in the few things and God will bless you as you continue to seek Him. The Bible says that Uzziah sought God and then the verse breaks and brings up a man whose name is Zechariah, one who had understanding in the visions of God. The amplified Bible reads that Zechariah instructed him in the things of God. Uzziah was king of the land but he had enough wisdom to humble himself and submit to the authority of one who understood the things of God. That takes humility to submit to someone who we think to be beneath us in status, education, wealth, etc. But Uzziah knew that having people around him who knew the Lord and understood the kingdom of God would be a major part in his success and prosperity. Let's thank the Lord for the Zechariahs in our lives.

II Chronicles 26: 6-7 "[6]And he went forth and warred against the Philistines, and brake down the wall of Gath, and the wall of Jabneh, and the wall of Ashdod, and built cities about Ashdod, and among the Philistines. [7]And God helped him against the Philistines, and against the Arabians that dwelt in Gurbaal, and the Mehunims." As long as Uzziah sought the Lord, God made him to prosper. King Uzziah yearned for God. The Bible speaks about seeking God first on many occasions and as a result He adds all things to us. Uzziah sought the Lord—he wanted more of God. He wanted God to reveal Himself to him in every way possible, as we should because in Him all fullness dwells. In Him there is meaning to our lives, there is joy, peace, prosperity, healing, wholeness and hope. There is a secret that God is about to reveal to you that will leave you from this day forward without excuse. Everything you need and want in life, God possesses it and if you possess Him these blessings will flow out of Him to you in ways you wouldn't believe. King Uzziah went forth and warred against the Philistines, and broke down many walls. These verses reveal his success in battle. Yes, you will go into battle and the enemy has built a fortress in your mind. He has caused division in your home, has stolen your joy and your peace, and now you must go to war to get those things back. The enemy will not lie down, but as with Uzziah, your success is guaranteed in the name of the Lord Jesus. God helped the king as He will with us, no matter how intense the battle may get, no matter how long it takes. If you hang in there you will win.

## Coast to Coast

II Chronicles 26:8 "And the Ammonites gave gifts to Uzziah: and his name spread abroad even to the entering in of Egypt; for he strengthened himself exceedingly." They brought gifts to the king. Who brought gifts? The neighbors, God will use people to bless you. When God is with you, it causes people to favor you and they just want to give you things and do things for you. Uzziah's name spread which means God made his name great which is a promise from (Gen. 12:2). Through God, he became international. Listen my sisters and brothers, that ministry, that organization, and that business you have that you want to grow and prosper, I dare you team up with the Lord, He will take you places, connect you with the right people, and teach you how to market. God will show you how to succeed. King Uzziah became strong, a very powerful man in the world because he was connected to God and God's plan for his life.

## Reach Out

II Chronicles 26:9-10 "⁹Moreover Uzziah built towers in Jerusalem at the corner gate, and at the valley gate, and at the turning of the wall, and fortified them." The man of God did not forget Jerusalem. The walls of Jerusalem had been broken down from the gate to the corner gate (II Chron. 25:23). To all of us who are walking with the Lord and God has caused us to succeed, use some of your money, your time, and your resources to help restore your hometown and build up your church. Don't forget the one who took you to the place that you are now enjoying. Reach out and do as Isaiah tells us in (Isaiah 61:4). Let's build the old waste, raise up the former desolations, repair the waste cities, the desolations of many generations. This is our duty as children of the Most High. We are blessed to be a blessing. "¹⁰Also he built towers in the desert, and digged many wells: for he had much cattle, both in the low country, and in the plains: husbandmen also, and vine dressers in the mountains, and in Carmel: for he loved husbandry." He had vine dressers, which tells me he was doing some hiring. People need jobs and you need someone to take care of all those possessions and land with which God has blessed you. The scripture tells us that King Uzziah loved farming. It is a blessing in life to be able to do exactly what you love doing. Some of us know that place. Others desire it but God says if we delight ourselves in Him, He will give us the desires of our heart. So the key is God, not the thing. If it is about Him, the things will come.

## We Need Them

II Chronicles 26:11-12 "[11]Moreover Uzziah had an host of fighting men, that went out to war by bands, according to the number of their account by the hand of Jeiel the scribe and Maaseiah the ruler, under the hand of Hananiah, one of the king's captains. [12]The whole number of the chief of the fathers of the mighty men of valour were two thousand and six hundred." Uzziah had a strong army. It is truly a blessing to have fighters around you, men and women who will stand and wage war against the enemy on your behalf, people who understand spiritual warfare, who will pray all night until they get a breakthrough, who know how to worship the Lord until every chain is broken, and until every stronghold has been torn down. An example is Abraham in Genesis 14:14 where he had the 318 trained servants that were ready for war at his command. This is the type of soldiers Uzziah had and no one could stand before them. I thank the Lord for the mighty men of valor that have been placed in my life.

II Chronicles 26:15 "[15]And he made in Jerusalem engines, invented by cunning men, to be on the towers and upon the bulwarks, to shoot arrows and great stones withal. And his name spread far abroad; for he was marvellously helped, till he was strong." God blessed King Uzziah to also have wise men around him—men who had knowledge, men that were creative. We don't have all the wisdom. And

I can honestly say that I have met some very smart men and women whose ideas and concepts and even whose inventions have helped me tremendously. So for those of you who think that God didn't give anybody else any understanding, skills, knowledge or wisdom, but you think He gave it all to you, you are selling yourself short. What arrogance to believe God gave it all to you, and when anyone else says anything you can't receive it. You need to repent and humble yourself. God took Uzziah all the way. He made him a force in the earth, He strengthened him, He established the man of God therefore, and King Uzziah lacked nothing. He was successful according to anyone's standard.

## Sudden Death

2 Chronicles 26:16 "16But when he was strong, his heart was lifted up to his destruction: for he transgressed against the LORD his God, and went into the temple of the LORD to burn incense upon the altar of incense." God had given Uzziah success on every level you can possibly imagine. And now the King thought he was untouchable; he thought he could defy the laws of God but he was sadly mistaken. God will not be mocked, insulted or have His precepts put aside. I want to admonish you my brothers and sisters that God will always bless those who diligently seek Him with all their hearts. Many of you allow your pride to get the best of you in one way or another and that can cause failure and severe setbacks in your lives.

As Uzziah's fame began to spread, his wealth increased and he became independent of God. This is happening in the world today. God uses your gifts and they bring you notoriety and fortune and then your hunger for God declines. You no longer hunger and thirst for Him anymore. You must be careful! The Bible says in 2 Chronicles 26:17-18, "[17]Azariah the priest went in after him, and with him fourscore priests of the LORD, that were valiant men: [18]And they withstood Uzziah the king, and said unto him, It appertaineth not unto thee, Uzziah, to burn incense unto the LORD, but to the priests the sons of Aaron, that are consecrated to burn incense: go out of the sanctuary; for thou hast trespassed; neither shall it be for thine honour from the LORD God." Here we see Uzziah doing things on his own. Pride has taken over. The Bible says pride goeth before destruction and a haughty spirit before a fall. Let's define haughty spirit—it means that one will not receive correction anymore. King Uzziah's pride got the best of him and his fall was sure to follow. Pride had come and the flesh had taken over. He went into the Holy place illegally and there was a price to be paid. Unfortunately, he paid it with his life. Uzziah is a perfect example of how God raises a person up and sets him in a position of authority. He started well like many of you do, but then he started acting as if he knew more than God. Being independent of the Lord is a place you don't want to be. Many have lost everything by thinking they can operate in their own authority and succeed. It is only by God's grace that you are not consumed and that you have received another chance to rise again. Uzziah died a leper which was a horrible and lonely death. His career, ministry and life were prosperous only with God at the wheel. Brothers and sisters, I encourage you to keep God at the wheel and you will succeed! With God, losing isn't optional.

# Chapter 10
# Plead Your Case

II Kings 20:1-3 "In those days was Hezekiah sick unto death. And the prophet Isaiah the son of Amoz came to him, and said unto him, Thus saith the LORD, Set thine house in order; for thou shalt die, and not live. Then he turned his face to the wall, and prayed unto the LORD, saying, I beseech thee, O LORD, remember now how I have walked before thee in truth and with a perfect heart, and have done that which is good in thy sight. And Hezekiah wept sore." Here is another example that we should follow as we shadow Christ. Let's first make this clear: God is no respecter of persons. He shows no partiality with His children. What He does for one, He will do for all who turn to him in faith. Hezekiah was the king of Israel at this time and the worst news he had ever heard had hit his front door. He had gotten sick and there was no cure for his sickness or disease. So God sent the prophet to tell him to get his affairs in order because he had come to the end of his life. Then Hezekiah began to pray to His God, the God he could always turn to when tragic or bad news came. Even though he had never been sick unto death, Hezekiah turned his face to the wall to pray because he depended on the integrity of God; His Word, His divine nature.

Turning to the wall was a sign that he had nowhere else to go but to God. He had money, he was the king, but his money or title couldn't erase this death sentence that was over his life. Sometimes in life you will have issues that money cannot buy and your friends, good looks and charm can't help. You will have to turn your face to the wall. You will have to close everything out, shut the door and pray to the Lord. I am not talking about any prayer. I'm talking about the prayer of faith which shall save the sick.

Hezekiah prays and pleads his case before God. How do we know it was a plea? When Hezekiah began to bring God to remembrance of His promises, he didn't embrace death, he did not prepare to die, and he did not throw a pity party—he reminded God of what he said in his Word. King Hezekiah began to tell God how he had walked before God in truth, in honesty, and integrity and that his heart was perfect before Him. This is key because God said He would show Himself strong on the behalf of those whose heart is perfect towards Him. Hezekiah makes it plain that he had done that which was good in God's sight. He was not a man pleaser. He didn't do what was right only when people were looking, and he didn't do good to seek accolades and pats on the back from men. He did what was right before the Lord. And that is important for you when you are talking about purpose in life and success in your prayer life. The Bible tells us to put God in remembrance; let us plead together; declare thou, that thou mayest be justified. So Hezekiah did just what God said in His word to do.

*Acts 10:39*
*James 5:1*
*II Chronicles 16:9*
*Isaiah 43:26*

# Chapter 11
# The Outcome

II Kings 20:4-6 Hezekiah's result was divine healing. Before Isaiah could get out of the middle court, the Word of the Lord came to him saying, "Turn again, and tell Hezekiah the captain of my people, Thus saith the LORD, the God of David thy father, I have heard thy prayer, I have seen thy tears: behold, I will heal thee: on the third day thou shalt go up unto the house of the LORD. And I will add unto thy days fifteen years; and I will deliver thee and this city out of the hand of the king of Assyria."

## A Quick Work

Now I know you are saying to yourself, "I've been praying forever for my healing and / or deliverance and it hasn't manifested." I can truly understand your pain and maybe a little confusion about how fast the Lord answered Hezekiah and it seems like forever with you. I have asked that question myself, and twirled it around in my mind for years, but during the process, I've discovered some awesome things about God. The vision is yet for an appointed time; though it tarries, wait for it. It will surely come to pass. If you have turned to the Word and have prayed according to the will of God which is the Word of God and you haven't experienced manifestation of the promise, be steadfast! God's Word is going to come to pass in your life. When you turn to the Word, you turn to the source from whom all blessings flow. Your healing is in the covenant; your breakthrough is in the covenant; your provision is in the covenant; and God says of His covenant that He will not break nor alter the thing that is gone out from His lips. What is God's covenant? God's covenant is His Word that goeth forth out of His lips. "All scripture is given by inspiration of God, and is profitable for doctrine, for reproof, for correction, for instruction in righteousness; That the man of God may be perfect, thoroughly furnished unto all good works." Take a look at the word inspiration in the Greek. It means "theopneustos," divinely breathed upon by God. And we see the word profitable, a word I love because it's what this book is about. In the Greek, profitable means "ophelimes," meaning advantageous. Webster's meaning is to be in a favorable position or factor, benefit or gain. And "NO" before you get it in your mind, God is not a Jack-in-the-Box. We don't just serve Him for gifts. But as the Word says, "Bless the LORD, O my soul, and forget not all His benefits." Profiting is just one of the many benefits of having God as your Father. Praise God!

Another benefit that God adds to us that's very important is that He will make us perfect and completely whole. Everyone desires to be complete. No one desires to live a life of lack, emptiness and barrenness. God says we will be thoroughly furnished, perfect, fully equipped meaning "exartizo" in Greek. I would liken it to a house that is fully furnished—all the chambers filled with all precious and pleasant riches.

God added fifteen years to Hezekiah's life. Anytime you turn to God, He adds to your life. So many of us at times feel as though God is taking things from us to teach us lessons but we must remember the Bible says the devil is a thief. God is not a thief. He gives us life and life more abundantly. He gave us His son. The devil will rob you and everything you have, but sadly we have been programmed to say that it was the Lord that took it all away. I pray that you would take notice on this day that God is into addition and multiplication.

*Habakkuk 2:3*
*Isaiah 55:11*
*Psalms 89:34*
*II Timothy 3:16-17*
*Proverbs 24:4*
*Psalms 103:2*
*John 10:10*

# Chapter 12
# The Ambassador

Daniel 6:16 "Then the king commanded, and they brought Daniel, and cast him into the den of lions. Now the king spake and said unto Daniel, Thy God whom thou servest continually, he will deliver thee." We all know the story of Daniel in the lions' den but it is so much more than a story that we read our children at bed times or that you teach in Sunday school. There are spiritual principles and truths that will change your life. Daniel was taken captive years ago by King Nebuchadnezzar but he was promoted to be over the whole realm because of his obedience to God. I want us to understand that we are as Daniel was in a foreign land. For the Bible says our citizenship is in Heaven. The Word also says that we are ambassadors in Christ Jesus. And as an ambassador of Christ, that means that we are just here on this earth as a representative of another nation or kingdom, and that kingdom's name is Heaven and Christ is the King. Heaven is where our citizenship lies.

Daniel lived by a different system than the men in Babylon. They reverenced material things. They worshipped idols, they prayed to human gods with limited strength and ability. Daniel was a man of integrity, a man who understood that the God of Abraham rules in the Heavens and had dominion in the affairs of His people's lives. Praise God! He had been challenged to compromise his integrity and his commitment to God on many occasions and he stood his ground. He held on to the Word of God.

*Philippians 3:30*
*II Corinthians 5:20*
*Psalms 75:5*
*Proverbs 3:4*

# Chapter 13
# Trap

Daniel was about to go through the test of his life. God had given Daniel favor in the sight of man and because of God's favor he was promoted to a very high position—a position under the King above all the presidents and princes of his day. When God's hand is upon your life, it brings jealously and envy, and envy breeds murder, so watch out! The other men in the region were envious and were seeking for a way to get rid of Daniel and they could not find a way unless they came against his faith in God. No, I'm not saying that Daniel was perfect, but he was blameless. He lived a life so committed to God that no one could blame or accuse him of anything. That's the life we should be leading before men. When people see us, it should be an outward expression of to Whom we serve and belong. There should be a distinction between the believer and the unbeliever.

Now the presidents and princes conspired against Daniel by going to the King with a new decree. When signing the decree, the King didn't know that it was a plot that the enemy was setting against Daniel. So King Nebuchadnezzar signed the decree that if any man prayed to any other god for thirty days he would be thrown into the lion's den. The enemy will go to great measures to stop the man of God. There is a conspiracy against you man of God! The decree was established and according to the law of the Medes and the Persians, it cannot be altered, meaning they could not revoke, cancel, or annul it. When Daniel knew that the writing was signed, he went into the house and began to pray and thank the Lord. Thanking the Lord was a part of Israel's ritual when praying. And though the decree had been signed, Daniel didn't stop his routine ceremonial. Trouble on the horizon didn't stop him from revering God because Daniel knew that his worship would release the angelic host of Heaven on his behalf because God loves a worshipper.

It seemed as though Daniel was committing suicide from a natural standpoint, but Daniel had a relationship with God and he knew that if he had to go in that lion's den that the Lord would see him through. Daniel walked with the Lord and the Lord had brought him through many trials and tribulations. He discovered some things about God on his journey and that one thing that was most important to him and to all of God's children was that no weapon that is formed against you shall prosper. That means exactly what it says. Yes, weapons will form, but they will not prosper against the children of God. We must, as Daniel did, turn to the Word. The Bible says, "Many are the afflictions of the righteous, but the Lord delivers them out of them all." Daniel knew that God would deliver him. God has never failed to do so. You also may be wondering why Daniel even had to go through this trial. The Lord has revealed to me that we have to go through trials because we are living in a fallen world. Satan is the principality of the air that works in the children of disobedience. He is forever at work through people trying to bring pain and discomfort to God's children and turn them against the Lord.

*Isaiah 54:17*
*Psalms 34:16*
*Ephesians 2:2*

# Chapter 14
# Unchanging Law

Now Daniel was caught praying and the presidents and princes went to the King, and the King has to go through with Daniel's punishment because of the decree that has been signed. The presidents and princes knew that the King had power to change any law except the law of the Medes and the Persians. King Nebuchadnezzar liked Daniel and he knew Daniel had done no wrong, but because he had signed the declaration, there was nothing the King could do but pray that Daniel's God would come through for him as he always did. The King wanted to help Daniel but he could not because the law has been set in stone. But praise God, there is another law called "The Book of the Law" which has the authority and power in both the heavenly and earthly realms. And no matter what happens, this law which is the Word of God will stand under and over anything that opposes it. There is no power stronger than God's Word and when you know and understand that, everyone around you will be losing sleep like the King did, but you will have peace because you know God's Word is omnipotent.

King Nebuchadnezzar brought a stone and laid it on the mouth of the den, and the King sealed it with his own signet. That meant that was over for Daniel; his death warrant had been signed. But I want to declare something to you about God. There may be something going on in your life that is beyond your control, a serious situation that's over your head, but God sits high and looks low; therefore, that situation is under Him. The devil may have said that your career is over; your prison sentence will never get overturned; your health will never get better; your children will become products of their environment, but I'm here to decree that no matter what the judge, doctor, lawyer, friends, or associates say, if they are not saying what God has already said and sealed with His blood, then it is a lie. That's why the Bible says, "Let God be true and every man a liar." I know they mean well and they are professionals and you have been trained to believe that tier professional opinions are right, but people will give you a death sentence based on their opinions and past experiences. When God is in it, peoples' opinions don't matter. It is only what God has decreed that matters. Even when it looks like the enemy has the upper hand, I dare you to believe God because He is perfecting that thing that is concerning you. Everything that concerns you, God is bringing it to perfection. That's why we can't quit because His Word is forever settled in Heaven. The process may look bad and it may feel bad, but as the Psalmist says, "Thou hast caused men to ride over our heads; we went through fire and through water: but thou broughtest us out into a wealthy place." So don't allow a symptom to tell you that you are not healed; don't allow a lawyer to tell you that you are defeated; don't allow an employer or supervisor to tell you that you will always be on this level; or allow a man to tell you that no one else wants you. Please my brothers and sisters don't allow these things to have significance in your life. We must be as Abraham was when he didn't consider his own body as being dead at 100 years old, nor the deadness of Sarah's womb. He staggered not at the promise of God with unbelief, but held strong in the faith, giving glory to God.

You must not even consider what man has said because if you do you will stagger at the promises of God. Let's look at what it means to consider. It means to take into consideration what one has said. The Greek word used here is "kataneo" which means to observe something fully. This is powerful because if you fully observe what is contrary to what God has said, you will begin to think defeat and it won't be long before you will be speaking defeat. And once that happens, you will be eating the fruit of what has been spoken.

*Romans 3:4*
*Psalms 138:1*

# Chapter 15
# Manifestation

Daniel 6:20-23 "And when he came to the den, he cried with a lamentable voice unto Daniel: and the king spake and said to Daniel, O Daniel, servant of the living God, is thy God, whom thou servest continually, able to deliver thee from the lions? [21]Then said Daniel unto the king, O king, live forever. [22]My God hath sent his angel, and hath shut the lions' mouths, that they have not hurt me: forasmuch as before him innocency was found in me; and also before thee, O king, have I done no hurt. [23]Then was the king exceedingly glad for him, and commanded that they should take Daniel up out of the den. So Daniel was taken up out of the den, and no manner of hurt was found upon him, because he believed in his God." The King made a very interesting statement when he said, "Thy God whom thou servest continuously." For God is God all the time. When things are good, He is God. When things are bad, He is God. The King saw Daniel serve God in winter, spring,

summer and fall. He also saw God do amazing things for Daniel. And the things he did not see, he heard about.

How many of you serve God continuously? Do you serve God through the dark places of life? Do you serve Him when things are delayed? Do you serve Him when the lights get turned off? Do you serve Him when there is no gas money or not even a car to put gas in? Will you serve God continuously is the question one must always ask themselves. Am I willing to go all the way with God?

Daniel tells the King that God has sent His angels to shut the mouth of the lions. The Bible says, "The angel of the LORD encampeth round about them that fear him, and delivereth them." Yes, we have angels protecting us from hurt, harm and dangers. We have angels on assignment for those who fear the Lord and they will deliver us out of any and all harm or danger seen and unseen. It is a blessing to know that I am not all alone on this journey. I don't have to fear anything because my salvation package came with bodyguards! Imagine these angels having enough power to close the mouth of hungry lions. What can man do unto you? This promise of angelic protection is predicated on the fact that Daniel had done no wrong. He was innocent before God. He was being obedient to what God had called him to do. Your obedience to God shows that you reverence Him and fear Him. And that causes God to act on your behalf in situations like this.

There are times in our lives where we may be in bad cities or neighborhoods. And in this day and time people are doing the craziest things. But it does us good to know that when it's late at night and we're leaving Wal-Mart alone or with our children, that we have angels encamped around us. And the angels are watching and protecting us to deliver us home safely. Praise God! Daniel was not hurt or injured in any way because he believed in his God. His faith was in God's power and His authority. His belief in God's power, promises, and purposes for Daniel's life played a major role in the outcome of this situation. It pays to believe in God, trusting that as you serve him continuously with all your heart and walk before Him in truth, you are secure. Nothing shall by any means harm you.

*Psalms 34:7*

## Not by Sight

I Kings 17:10-14 "So he arose and went to Zarephath. And when he came to the gate of the city, behold, the widow woman was there gathering of sticks: and he called to her, and said, Fetch me, I pray thee, a little water in a vessel, that I may drink. ¹¹And as she was going to fetch it, he called to her, and said, Bring me, I pray thee, a morsel of bread in thine hand. ¹²And she said, As the LORD thy God liveth, I have not a cake, but an handful of meal in a barrel, and a little oil in a cruse: and, behold, I am gathering two sticks, that I may go in and dress it for me and my son, that we may eat it, and die. ¹³And Elijah said unto her, Fear not; go and do as thou hast said: but make me thereof a little cake first, and bring it unto me, and after make for thee and for thy son. For thus saith the

LORD God of Israel, The barrel of meal shall not waste, neither shall the cruse of oil fail, until the day that the LORD sendeth rain upon the earth. " In the passage, we have a situation where there's a famine in the land. Israel is being punished for their sins. Note where sin dwells continually, a drought is sure to follow in due time. The Bible says in Ecclesiastes 8:6, "Because to every purpose there is time and judgment, therefore the misery of man is great upon him." The good thing is that this law works also when you are doing good, and blessings are sure to follow you all the days of your life. This is a promise that was true for David and it true for us as well.

Now we have a widow, her son, and God's prophet. The widow represents the believer, the prophet, Elijah, represents God's vessel, a messenger from God, and the boy represents the family of the believer. Elijah arrived on the property of the widow as she was gathering sticks. We can assume that she was poor because she had no help, no servants, and the famine had taken its toll on the land. She was preparing to bake her last piece of bread when the man of God came with a word from the Lord. The widow then knew that her day for a miracle had come. As Shirley Caesar says, "…She was next in line for a miracle." As believers, we must know that God is concerned about us and He has a set time in which he is going to release a miracle into our lives. A miracle is something supernatural where God intervenes in your life and things happen out of the ordinary—things you cannot explain. And it's something nobody can do for you but God!

The man of God called the widow and said, "Give me a little water in a vessel that I may drink." Then as she was going about, he said, "Bring me some bread, also." Now from the looks of it, it seems as though Elijah had come to take from the widow instead of giving. But as always, God is teaching us something about His principles. The Lord instills values about the Kingdom of God that many in the world don't understand or comprehend. In this passage, He is about to teach us about walking by faith and not by sight. So she began to speak from a natural perspective like most of us do when we are asked to do something against the ordinary. The natural mind doesn't understand the things of the spirit so we must be taught. Now this widow was about to go to class; she was about to learn what it meant to walk by faith. She said, "As the Lord your God lives, I have not a cake, but a handful of meal in a barrel and a little oil in a cruse; and behold I am gathering two sticks, that I may go in and dress it for me and my son, that we may eat and die." She sounds just like us when it comes to God and the things of God. We profess Christianity but we have fear and trust issues in certain areas and a lot of times with good reason. A bad economy, low paying jobs, working for a temp service, you may be the only one in the house working, or maybe you just don't understand what the Bible may be saying concerning certain issues, or you could be tired of giving to people all the time. Believe me, I understand.

The man of God, Elijah, said, "Fear not; go and do as thou hast said: but make me thereof a little cake first, and bring it unto me, and after make for thee and for thy son." Elijah says not to fear because he knows that fear will paralyze your movement; causing you not to respond immediately when the Spirit speaks. God has not given us the spirit of fear. The Bible says fear brings torment, and in a situation like this where there is a drought and this is the last meal, she has to move fear out and bring in all faith. This is a situation where all faith is needed. That is why in the Bible when God challenges His people to step out on faith and do great exploits, He has to assure them that He is with them, therefore, they should not fear. He knows fear will keep you from walking by faith.

### God First

The next thing Elijah said was "give me mine's first." He had the audacity to let that come out of his mouth knowing that she has a son to feed. But stay focused! God must be number one in our lives. He says "seek ye first the Kingdom of God and his righteousness and all these things will be added unto you." Abel brought the firstling of the flock and his offering was accepted over Cain's. The Word says, "Honour the LORD with thy substance, and with the firstfruits of all thine increase." This is called "God's Way"—God will not play second string in your life. If you try to bring Him off the bench when your way doesn't work, that decision will set you back! Let's get it right the first time. This book is about showing us how to get it right with God the first time so that you can prosper and succeed. The principle here is God over everyone and everything, no exceptions! Let's go a bit further so that I can show you what else I love about God's plan and God's way. He attaches a promise to everything He asks of us.

"For thus saith the LORD God of Israel, The barrel of meal shall not waste, neither shall the cruse of oil fail, until the day that the LORD sendeth rain upon the earth." He says the God of Israel because there are many gods in the world, but there is only one true God who is faithful and consistent in nature and character, and that is the God of Israel. Elijah tells her that her jar of meal shall not waste, neither shall the cruse of oil fail. In Hebrew, the word fail means "chacer," meaning to lack, decrease, and lessen.

God is saying if you give my prophet some water and bread first, you will not lack. Let's go to Matthews 10:42 (AMP) "And whoever gives to one of these little ones [in rank or influence] even a cup of cold water because he is My disciple, surely I declare to you, he shall not lose his reward." Of course she didn't have Matthew to go to as we do, so she had to move in faith in the drought and she did as Elijah said. And she and her household ate for many days. The jar of meal was not spent nor did the bottle of oil fail according to the word which the Lord spoke through Elijah. The Lord spoke a word through the prophet but it's up to us to decide which way we are going to go.

*Matthew 6:33*
*Genesis 4:4*
*Proverbs 3:9*

## Life or Death

Deuteronomy 30:19 "I call heaven and earth to record this day against you, that I have set before you life and death, blessing and cursing: therefore choose life, that both thou and thy seed may live." Mankind has made many decisions based on emotions, ignorance or just wrong information. Their decisions have brought curses instead of blessings on their life; death instead of life. We are eating the fruit of our own way. Jeremiah 10:23 says, "O LORD, I know that the way of man is not in himself: it is not in man that walketh to direct his steps." But yet we continue to make choices independent of God as if we know what we are doing and then we blame the Lord. Proverbs 19:3 says, "The foolishness of man perverteth his way: and his heart fretteth against the LORD." This scripture is saying that man does his own things and turns the blame on God. But God says I set before you life and death, blessings and curses, and He encourages us to choose life so that we and our dependents may live and live life more abundantly. The choices we make affect not just us but everyone in close proximity of us. If the widow had made a bad choice, the outcome would have been different, affecting not only her, but her son as well. Because she sewed a seed into the man of God, God in turn multiplied the seed that was sown. Praise God! *(II Corinthians 9:10 Now he that ministereth seed to the sower both minister bread for your food, and multiply your seed sown, and increase the fruits of your righteousness.)*

Miracles and blessings are attached to obeying God. Isaiah says if we are willing and obedient, we shall eat the good of the land!